D0382412

ONE POT

ONE POT

PERFECTLY PREPARED TO ENJOY EVERY DAY

This edition published in 2012

LOVE FOOD is an imprint of Parragon Books Ltd

Parragon
Chartist House
15–17 Trim Street
Bath, BA1 1HA, UK

Copyright © Parragon Books Ltd 2012

LOVE FOOD and the accompanying heart device is a registered trademark of Parragon Books Ltd in Australia, the UK, USA, India, and the EU.

www.parragon.com/lovefood

All rights reserved. No part of this publication may be reproduced, stored in a retrieval system, or transmitted, in any form or by any means, electronic, mechanical, photocopying, recording, or otherwise, without the prior permission of the copyright holder.

ISBN: 978-1-78186-726-6

Printed in China

Concept: Patrik Jaros & Günter Beer
Recipes and food styling: Patrik Jaros www.foodlook.com
Text: Günter Beer, Gerhard von Richthofen, Patrik Jaros, Jörg Zipprick
Photography: Günter Beer www.beerfoto.com
Photographer's assistants: Sigurd Buchberger, Aranxa Alvarez
Cook's assistants: Magnus Thelen, Johannes von Bemberg
Designed by Estudio Merino www.estudiomerino.com
Produced by Buenavista Studio s.l. www.buenavistastudio.com
The visual index is a registered design of Buenavista Studio s.l. (European Trademark Office number 000252796-001)
Project management: trans texas publishing, Cologne
Typesetting: Nazire Ergün, Cologne

Notes for the Reader
This book uses standard kitchen measuring spoons and cups. All spoon and cup measurements are level unless otherwise indicated. Unless otherwise stated, milk is assumed to be whole, butter is assumed to be salted, eggs are large, individual vegetables are medium, and pepper is freshly ground black pepper. Unless otherwise stated, all root vegetables should be washed and peeled before using.

For the best results, use a meat thermometer when cooking meat and poultry—check the latest USDA government guidelines for current advice.

Garnishes and serving suggestions are all optional and not necessarily included in the recipe ingredients or method. The times given are only an approximate guide. Preparation times differ according to the techniques used by different people and the cooking times may also vary from those given. Optional ingredients, variations, or serving suggestions have not been included in the calculations.

Recipes using raw or very lightly cooked eggs should be avoided by infants, the elderly, pregnant women, and people with weakened immune systems. Pregnant and breast-feeding women are advised to avoid eating peanuts and peanut products. People with nut allergies should be aware that some of the prepared ingredients used in the recipes in this book may contain nuts. Always check the packaging before use.

Picture acknowledgments
All photos by Günter Beer, Barcelona

Contents

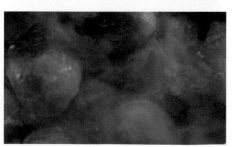

Introduction

If you don't like raiding your cupboards and battling with several pots and pans to produce one meal, this is just the right book for you. Although a variety of saucepans, skillets, casserole dishes, woks, and pie plates are used to cook the delicious dishes in this book, you'll need only one cooking vessel for any of the recipes! You won't have the hassle of matching saucepans with lids or working on limited stove-top rings—and you won't have to worry about washing up piles of dirty pots and pans after your meal.

Using just one cooking vessel has other advantages. It's easy, and it saves both energy and time because either the dish cooks quickly in a wok or skillet, or it stews slowly in the oven in a casserole dish or pie pan, so you can get on with other things in the meantime. And don't underestimate the flavor in these one-dish meals. All the ingredients cook together in their own juices and develop their own unique and delicious aroma.

If you think only soups or stews can be cooked in one pot, you will be amazed at the diversity of our one-dish suggestions. The choice of recipes in this book includes vegetarian dishes as well as meat, fish, and seafood recipes. We feature soups and stews, curries, ragouts, and rice and pasta dishes, including international specialties and culinary classics, some warm and hearty, some exotic and spicy.

The spectrum of countries whose culinary traditions we sample ranges from Hungary (goulash), Spain (paella), Italy (risotto), and Ireland (Irish Stew) to India (biryani) and Vietnam (beef with ginger), and even include our own (squash soup). There are wholesome dishes, such as Tomato Bean Stew with Spicy Lamb Sausage and Sour Vegetable & Lentil Stew, alongside more refined cuisine for special occasions or the adventurous, such as Stuffed Pigeons Wrapped in Bacon, Lobster Bisque, and Duck Breast with Orange-Pepper Sauce.

Pots, pans, and other cooking vessels

Every household is equipped with pots and pans and a skillet. It's also useful to invest in a casserole dish, roaster, and wok. Choose good-quality items. Pots and pans should be a reasonable weight and have a thick bottom that will conduct the heat well and prevent the contents from burning. Make sure you choose the right size for your recipe. If the saucepan is too small, the contents will cook unevenly and cannot be stirred properly. However, in an oversize pan, the liquid will evaporate too quickly and the food will probably burn. The most frequently used cooking vessels are the following:

Pie plates and gratin dishes: These heat-resistant dishes are ideal for gratins and other oven-cooked dishes. Flameproof ones can be used on the stove top.

Roasters: A large pan with a heavy lid for cooking meat. A roaster is ideal for preparing larger pieces of meat or poultry that are cooked whole. They are usually big enough to cook vegetables in, too. Roasting in the juices of the meat, they develop a wonderful flavor.

Casserole dish: A casserole dish with a lid or covered with aluminum foil is ideal for preparing dishes that simmer for a long time in the oven or, if flameproof, on the stove. When covered, ingredients can develop their full flavors.

Paella pan: A large, flat pan in which the classic Spanish dish is prepared. A conventional deep sauté pan, however, can also be used.

Wok: A conical cooking pot with a round bottom. The wok gets hottest in the center. Ingredients are cooked here or pushed aside as required. Woks are usually used to stir-fry vegetables and meat. They are available with two handles or a single handle on one side. If you have an electric stove top, you'll need a wok with a flat bottom.

Other cooking utensils

Wooden spoon: With a wooden spoon, you can stir ingredients easily without damaging the bottom of your pot or pan. This is especially important if the pan has a nonstick or enamel coating.

Spatula: A spatula is particularly useful for turning over and lifting out certain food items, such as pancakes, and can also be used for stirring.

Meat fork: Larger pieces of meat can be turned and, if required, removed from a pan with a meat fork.

Slotted spoon: A slotted spoon can be used to skim excess fat from the top of stews and casseroles, or to drain the excess liquid from meat and vegetables when serving straight from the pot.

Ingredients

There is virtually nothing that cannot be cooked in a single pot. However, a number of rules should be observed:

If the dish is prepared with meat or poultry, sear these briefly before adding the other ingredients. The meat cooks more quickly in this way and you will have a tasty, aromatic gravy.

Different ingredients require different cooking times. Generally speaking, harder ingredients take longer to cook and should be added first, and softer ingredients should be added later.

Leafy greens should be cooked only briefly so that they stay crisp and retain their bright color. This will also prevent them from overpowering the flavor of the other vegetables. Dried beans should be soaked overnight and boiled for at least 10 minutes, then drained and rinsed, before being added to the pan.

Homemade stock, of course, tastes best. If you're in a hurry or balk at the effort involved in preparing your own, instant products are a good alternative. However, do make sure the stock is not too salty. There are numerous high-quality instant products available today, ranging from bouillon cubes to cartons of fresh stock.

Alcohol can enhance the flavor of many casseroles and stews, but do make sure that it reaches boiling point and that you cook it off for a few minutes. The liquid will reduce, leaving a wonderfully rich gravy or sauce.

How to use this book

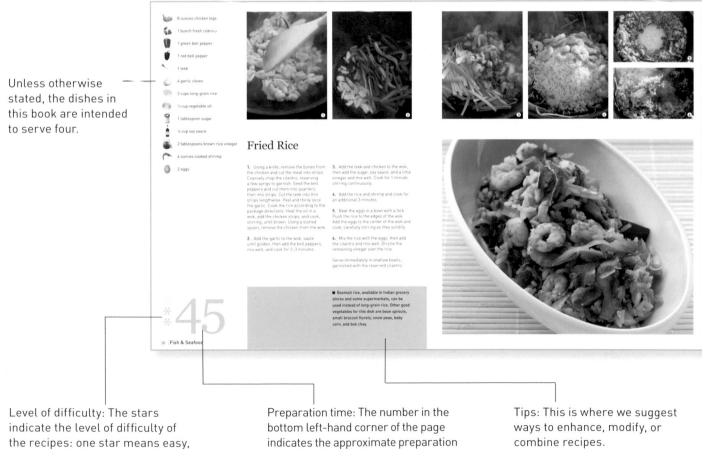

Unless otherwise stated, the dishes in this book are intended to serve four.

8 ounces chicken legs
1 bunch fresh cilantro
1 green bell pepper
1 red bell pepper
1 leek
4 garlic cloves
2 cups long-grain rice
½ cup vegetable oil
1 tablespoon sugar
¼ cup soy sauce
2 tablespoons brown rice vinegar
4 ounces cooked shrimp
2 eggs

Fried Rice

1. Using a knife, remove the bones from the chicken and cut the meat into strips. Coarsely chop the cilantro, reserving a few sprigs to garnish. Seed the bell peppers and cut them into quarters, then into strips. Cut the leek into thin strips lengthwise. Peel and thinly slice the garlic. Cook the rice according to the package directions. Heat the oil in a wok, add the chicken strips, and cook, stirring, until brown. Using a slotted spoon, remove the chicken from the wok.

2. Add the garlic to the wok, sauté until golden, then add the bell peppers, mix well, and cook for 2–3 minutes.

3. Add the leek and chicken to the wok, then add the sugar, soy sauce, and a little vinegar and mix well. Cook for 1 minute, stirring continuously.

4. Add the rice and shrimp and cook for an additional 3 minutes.

5. Beat the eggs in a bowl with a fork. Push the rice to the edges of the wok. Add the eggs to the center of the wok and cook, carefully stirring as they solidify.

6. Mix the rice with the eggs, then add the cilantro and mix well. Drizzle the remaining vinegar over the rice.

Serve immediately in shallow bowls, garnished with the reserved cilantro.

■ Basmati rice, available in Indian grocery stores and some supermarkets, can be used instead of long-grain rice. Other good vegetables for this dish are bean sprouts, small broccoli florets, snow peas, baby corn, and bok choy.

※ *※* 45

30 : Fish & Seafood

Level of difficulty: The stars indicate the level of difficulty of the recipes: one star means easy, two intermediate, three difficult.

Preparation time: The number in the bottom left-hand corner of the page indicates the approximate preparation time in minutes.

Tips: This is where we suggest ways to enhance, modify, or combine recipes.

¼ cup olive oil

2 tablespoons sugar

2 celery stalks, finely diced

2 carrots, finely diced

1 onion, finely diced

2 garlic cloves

4 cloves

2 strips lemon peel

1 teaspoon white peppercorns, crushed

1 fresh rosemary sprig

1 fresh thyme sprig

1 bay leaf

1 tablespoon tomato paste

11 tomatoes (about 2¾ pounds), quartered

1 teaspoon salt

3 cups chicken stock

Tomato Soup with Basil Croutons

1. Pour the oil into a large saucepan. Add the sugar, celery, carrots, and onions and gently sauté for 5 minutes. Peel the garlic cloves, cut in half, and add to the pan with the cloves, lemon peel, peppercorns, rosemary, thyme, and bay leaf. Sauté for an additional 5 minutes.

2. Add the tomato paste and sauté for 1 minute, then add the tomatoes and salt.

3. Pour in the stock and bring to a boil over high heat. Reduce the heat to medium and simmer for 20 minutes.

4. Remove what is left of the herb sprigs and the bay leaf and puree the ingredients in the pan for 1 minute, using an immersion blender.

5. Using a ladle, pour the soup through a fine strainer, pushing it through until the remnants are almost dry. This binds the soup and enhances the flavor.

Transfer the soup to warm bowls and serve with basil croutons.

■ For the basil croutons, melt 1½ tablespoons butter in a nonstick skillet, add 1 cup cubed white bread and sauté, stirring continuously, until golden brown. Add 4 basil leaves, cut into ribbons, season with salt, and mix together. Remove the croutons from the heat to prevent them from burning and set aside in a bowl until needed.

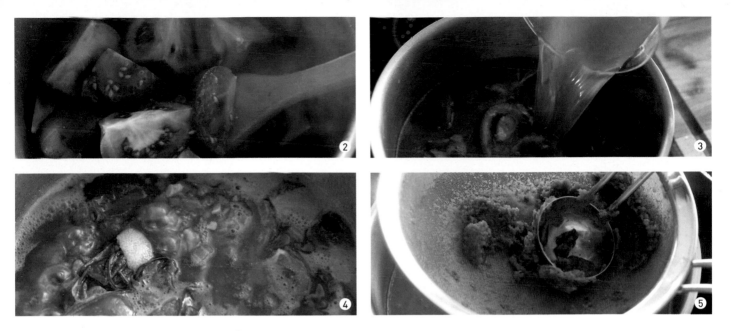

3½ pounds winter squash

½ bunch fresh dill

½-inch piece fresh ginger

1 garlic clove

1 large carrot

1 red bell pepper

1 celery stalk

1 small onion

3 tablespoons butter

salt, to taste

freshly grated nutmeg, to taste

3 cloves

1 bay leaf

1 teaspoon ketchup

½ teaspoon curry powder

1½ teaspoons sweet paprika

4 cups chicken stock

1 cup cream

½ cup crème fraîche or sour cream

Squash Soup with Cheese Croutons

1. Cut the top off the squash from about 1¼ inches down. Scrape out the seeds with a spoon. Finely chop the dill and set aside.

2. Using a melon baller, scoop out the flesh from the squash and the top, without damaging the skin. Leave about a ½-inch-thick wall. Reserve the flesh.

3. Peel the ginger and garlic and thinly slice. Cut the carrots, red bell pepper, celery, and onion into ½-inch pieces. Melt the butter in a large saucepan, add the garlic and onion, and cook over low heat until translucent. Add the carrots, red bell pepper, celery, and ginger and cook for an additional 5 minutes.

4. Add the squash flesh. Season with salt and nutmeg, then add the cloves and bay leaf. Cook over medium heat for about 10 minutes, until the squash begins to fall apart easily. Push it to the edges of the pan.

5. Add the ketchup, curry powder, and paprika to the center of the pan and cook for 1 minute, then mix in the squash.

6. Pour in the stock, bring to a boil, and simmer over medium heat for 15 minutes. Add the cream and crème fraîche and bring back to a boil.

■ For the cheese croutons, cut half a baguette into ¼-inch thick slices, sprinkle with ½ cup shredded Gouda cheese or Swiss cheese and bake in a preheated oven at 400°F for 5 minutes, or until the cheese has melted.

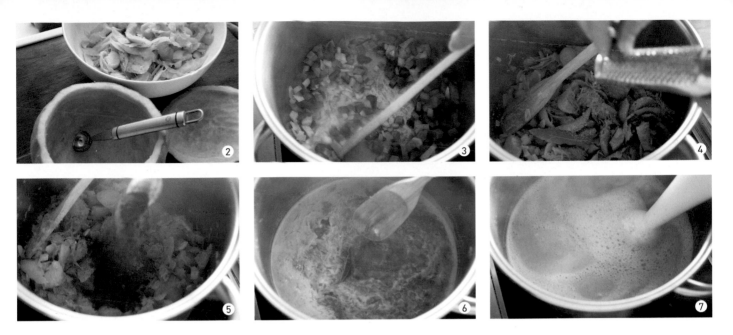

7. Puree with an immersion blender for 1 minute, then pass it through a fine strainer. Use a ladle to press the liquid out of the remnants.

Pour the soup into the hollowed-out squash, sprinkle with the reserved dill, and serve with the cheese croutons.

2¾ cups dried chickpeas

2 onions

1 small eggplant

3 garlic cloves

2 tomatoes

⅓ cup sunflower oil

1 tablespoon star anise seeds

6 cardamom pods

8 cloves

1 cinnamon stick

salt and pepper, to taste

1 teaspoon ground coriander

1 teaspoon ground turmeric

6 cups water or vegetable stock

1 cup plain yogurt

pinch of ground cinnamon

few drops of lemon juice

2 fresh mint sprigs, shredded

①

Indian Chickpea Curry with Cinnamon Yogurt & Mint

1. Soak the chickpeas in cold water for at least 2 hours. Finely dice the onions. Cut the eggplant into ¾-inch pieces. Peel the garlic and thinly slice. Peel the tomatoes and cut them into quarters. Heat the oil in a large saucepan over medium heat, add the garlic, and cook until golden brown. Add the star anise seeds, cardamom pods, cloves, and cinnamon stick and sauté for 2–3 minutes.

2. Add the onions, cook until translucent, then push to the side of the pan. Add the eggplant to the center of the pan, season with salt and pepper and sauté for 5 minutes.

3. Sprinkle with the coriander and turmeric and cook for 5 minutes, until the onions and eggplant are slightly mushy. Drain and rinse the soaked chickpeas.

4. Add the chickpeas to the pan and cook for an additional 5 minutes, then add the tomatoes and water.

5. Cover with a lid and simmer over medium heat for 1 hour 10 minutes. The chickpeas should remain submerged. Mix the yogurt with the ground cinnamon, lemon juice, and mint.

Serve in bowls with the yogurt mix on the side.

+ 2 hours' soaking

■ If possible, soak the chickpeas overnight. They will soften faster while cooking. Drain and rinse in fresh water before adding to the pan.

1 carrot

2 celery stalks, plus leaves to garnish

1 leek

1 onion

2 tablespoons oil

1 tablespoon butter

1 tablespoon tomato paste

1¼ cups lentils, rinsed and drained

⅔ cup white wine

2 cups stock

salt and pepper

½ teaspoon dried marjoram

2 tablespoons vinegar

2 teaspoons Dijon mustard

2 fresh parsley sprigs, chopped

Sour Vegetable & Lentil Stew

1. Finely dice the carrot, celery, and leek, reserving a few celery leaves to garnish. Dice the onion.

2. Heat the oil and butter in a large saucepan over high heat, add the vegetables, and sauté, then add the tomato paste and stir.

3. Add the lentils to the vegetables and sauté.

4. Add the wine and bring to a boil. Add the stock and simmer for 25–30 minutes.

5. Season with salt and pepper and stir in the marjoram. Add the vinegar and mustard.

Stir in the chopped parsley before serving and garnish with the chopped celery leaves.

■ This is an outstanding side dish with broiled fish, or it can be served with a few crispy bacon strips. The lentils can also be rounded off with finely chopped anchovies or capers, or even a little sour cream.

½ teaspoon caraway seeds

4½ tablespoons vegetable oil

1 pound seitan or tofu

1 garlic clove, chopped

1 teaspoon chopped fresh marjoram

salt and pepper, to taste

3 onions

4 Yukon Gold potatoes, peeled and cubed

2 tablespoons sweet paprika

4 cups vegetable stock

1 teaspoon snipped fresh chives, to garnish

1

Vegetarian Goulash with Potatoes & Paprika

1. Drizzle the caraway seeds with some of the oil and finely chop. The oil helps the seeds to stay on the cutting board.

2. Cut the seitan into cubes. Mix together the garlic, caraway seeds, and marjoram in a bowl, then season with salt and pepper. Add the seitan and let marinate for 10 minutes.

3. Heat the remaining oil in a large saucepan. Slice the onions into strips, add to the pan, and sauté, then add the potatoes.

4. Dust with the paprika and stir well.

5. Add the marinated seitan to the potatoes and mix.

6. Add the stock and simmer for about 30 minutes.

Transfer to bowls, sprinkle with chives, and serve.

* * * **50**

■ Adding other vegetables, such as red and yellow bell peppers, zucchini, and diced tomatoes, adds zest to the goulash and gives it a fresh and fruity flavor. Seitan, found in health food stores, is a tasty substitute for beef or pork. If you like goulash really hot, replace half the sweet paprika with hot paprika.

2 bacon strips

2 tomatoes

1 garlic clove

1 shallot

6 artichokes

5 tablespoons salted butter

¼ cup olive oil

pinch of sugar

salt and pepper, to taste

1⅓ cups risotto rice

3 cups chicken stock

2 fresh rosemary sprigs

1 cup freshly grated
Parmesan cheese

fresh flat-leaf parsley sprigs,
to garnish

Tomato & Artichoke Risotto

1. Cut the bacon into ½-inch-wide strips. Peel the tomatoes and cut them into ½-inch pieces. Finely chop the garlic and shallot. Cut the artichokes into sixths.

2. Heat 2 tablespoons of the butter and 2 tablespoons of the oil in a nonstick skillet until foaming, then add the shallot and garlic and cook until translucent. Add the tomatoes, and sugar, season with salt and pepper, and simmer for about 2 minutes.

3. Add the rice and stir with a wooden spoon, then add the stock until the rice is just covered. The risotto should only be tossed from now on, not stirred. Simmer the risotto for about 15–18 minutes, adding the remaining hot stock gradually.

4. Meanwhile, heat the remaining oil in a separate nonstick skillet, add the artichokes, and rosemary, season with salt and pepper, and gently sauté for about 5 minutes.

5. Add the bacon and sauté until crisp. Remove the rosemary and add the artichokes and bacon to the risotto. Add the Parmesan cheese and the remaining butter and stir.

Transfer to deep bowls and serve immediately, garnished with parsley.

■ **Mushroom risotto:** Clean 8 ounces of mushrooms and cut into quarters or sixths (about 3½ cups). Heat 2 tablespoons of olive oil in a nonstick skillet, add the mushrooms, and sauté for 5 minutes, until light brown. Season with salt and pepper. Peel half a garlic clove, finely chop, and add to the mushrooms. Finely chop the leaves of half a bunch of parsley and add to the garlic and mushrooms. Drizzle the juice of half a lemon over the mushroom mixture, then transfer to the risotto at the end of Step 2. Stir in 1 cup of freshly grated Parmesan cheese and serve immediately.

2 red bell peppers

1 green bell pepper

3 small onions

4 Yukon gold potatoes

2 garlic cloves

rind of 1 lemon

½ teaspoon caraway seeds

3 tablespoons vegetable oil

2 teaspoons ground sweet paprika

salt and pepper, to taste

5 cups vegetable stock

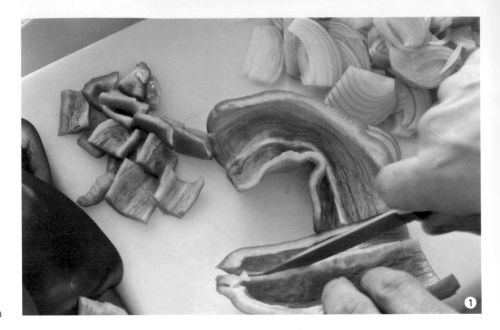

Vegetable Goulash

1. Halve and seed the red and green bell peppers and cut them into ¾-inch pieces. Roughly dice the onions. Peel the potatoes, cut into ¾-inch pieces, and set aside, covered with cold water. Peel the garlic cloves and finely chop with the lemon rind. Prepare the caraway seeds by drizzling some oil on them and then chopping them.

2. Heat the oil in a large saucepan, then add the onions and sauté. Drain the potato pieces in a colander. Add the potatoes to the pan and sauté gently for 5 minutes.

3. Sprinkle the garlic, lemon rind, caraway seeds, and paprika over the potatoes and onions, and gently sauté.

4. Add the bell peppers, season with salt and pepper, and cook for a few minutes over medium heat.

5. Pour in the stock and simmer for about 25 minutes, stirring occasionally.

Ladle the goulash into deep bowls and serve with rye bread.

■ Diced zucchini and whole cherry tomatoes can be used instead of the bell peppers.

* * * **55**

½ head broccoli (medium)

1 green bell pepper

1 garlic clove

8 ounces rice noodles

2 large green chiles

⅓ cup vegetable oil

2 tablespoons Thai fish sauce

2 tablespoons soy sauce

1 tablespoon sugar

2 eggs, beaten

1 tablespoon toasted sesame seeds, to garnish

Rice Noodles with Broccoli & Green Chiles

1. Cut off the broccoli florets. Halve, core, and seed the green bell pepper and thinly slice into 2-inch strips. Finely chop the garlic.

2. Cook the rice noodles according to the package directions, then refresh them under cold running water and let drain. Slice the chiles into thin rings.

3. Heat a large wok over high heat. Add 3 tablespoons of the oil, then add the broccoli and sauté for about 5 minutes, stirring frequently. Add the fish sauce, then remove the broccoli and set aside.

4. Add the remaining oil to the wok, then add the garlic and sauté. Add the noodles, then add the green bell pepper. Add the soy sauce and sprinkle with the sugar.

5. Return the broccoli to the wok and stir. Slowly add the eggs to the side of the wok and stir into the mixture. Add the chile rings.

Transfer to deep bowls, sprinkle with sesame seeds, and serve immediately.

*****40**

■ Other fresh garnishes and herbs, such as chives, Thai basil, cilantro, or bean sprouts, also complement this dish.

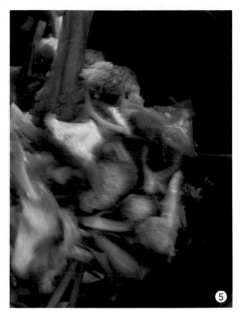

1 onion

3 shallots

1 large carrot

2 celery stalks

3 garlic cloves

10 black peppercorns

2¾-pound cooked lobster

3 tablespoons olive oil

1 stick butter

2 fresh thyme sprigs,
coarsely chopped

1 fresh rosemary sprig,
coarsely chopped

2 bay leaves, coarsely chopped

4 (14½-ounce) cans chopped plum
tomatoes

1 tablespoon short-grain rice

¼ cup dry vermouth,
or ¼ cup cognac

⅔ cup white wine

4 cups shellfish stock

1¾ cups cream

2 basil leaves

salt, to taste

cayenne pepper, to taste

①

Lobster Bisque

1. Cut the onion, shallots, carrot, and celery into ¼-inch pieces. Crush the garlic in its skin. Crush the peppercorns with a knife. Crack open the lobster and reserve the flesh. Heat the oil in a wide saucepan, then add the lobster shells and sauté for about 5 minutes. Add the butter and continue to sauté.

2. Add the chopped vegetables, garlic, peppercorns, and chopped herbs, and cook until translucent. Scrape any residue from the bottom of the pan to prevent it from burning.

3. Add the tomatoes and cook. Add the rice, vermouth, and wine, bring to a boil and cook for an additional 5 minutes, until the alcohol evaporates.

4. Pour in the shellfish stock and simmer for 20 minutes.

5. Add the cream and basil and simmer for an additional 1 minute. Carefully blend the soup with an immersion blender on the lowest speed. Using a ladle, pass the soup through a fine strainer into a clean saucepan, squeezing out the shells. Bring back to a boil and season with salt and cayenne pepper.

Serve the soup in deep bowls, dividing the reserved lobster flesh among the bowls.

✳
✳
✳ **70**

■ Many high-end grocers now carry a "lobster paste" which can be diluted to create a delicious stock—this is a handy alternative if you cannot use lobster shells.

3 shallots

1½ celery stalks

1 leek

1 garlic clove

2 tablespoons butter

2 bay leaves

1 fresh thyme sprig

salt and pepper, to taste

4½ pounds mussels, cleaned and debearded

⅔ cup white wine

½ bunch fresh parsley, finely chopped

Mussels Steamed in White Wine

1. Peel the shallots and cut into fine strips. Slice the celery and leek into fine strips. Press the garlic clove in its skin. Melt the butter in a saucepan. Add the garlic and shallots, then add the bay leaves, thyme, celery, and leek and sauté briefly. Season with salt and pepper. Discard any mussels with broken shells and any that refuse to close when tapped.

2. Add the mussels and mix with the vegetables. Pour in the wine, cover the pan, and let simmer for 3–5 minutes, until the mussels open. Discard any mussels that remain closed. Sprinkle the parsley over the mussels.

Mix well and serve immediately.

30

■ Use an empty mussel shell to eat the cooked mussels without cutlery.

1½ pounds fresh peas
in their pods

2 red bell peppers

2 green bell peppers

⅓ cup extra virgin olive oil

5 cups short-grain rice

3 cups white wine

salt and pepper, to taste

pinch of ground saffron

4½ pounds mixed fish
and seafood

9 cups chicken stock

Spanish Paella

1. Shell the peas. Seed and dice the red and green bell peppers.

2. Heat the oil in a paella pan, add the diced bell peppers and the rice, and cook over medium heat, stirring. Add the wine and season with salt and pepper. Sprinkle with saffron.

3. Discard any mussels or clams with broken shells and any that refuse to close when tapped. Add the fish and seafood to the rice.

4. Pour in the stock, add the peas, and cook for about 20 minutes. Discard any mussels or clams that remain closed.

Serve directly from the paella pan.

This paella will serve 6–8 people.

■ Use Spanish short-grain rice for best results. Italian short-grain rice, such as risotto rice, could make the dish thick and rich. Chicken or rabbit meat can be used in place of the fish, to accompany the seafood.

8 ounces chicken legs

1 bunch fresh cilantro

1 green bell pepper

1 red bell pepper

1 leek

4 garlic cloves

2 cups long-grain rice

⅓ cup vegetable oil

1 tablespoon sugar

¼ cup soy sauce

2 tablespoons brown rice vinegar

4 ounces cooked shrimp

2 eggs

Fried Rice

1. Using a knife, remove the bones from the chicken and cut the meat into strips. Coarsely chop the cilantro, reserving a few sprigs to garnish. Seed the bell peppers and cut them into quarters, then into strips. Cut the leek into thin strips lengthwise. Peel and thinly slice the garlic. Cook the rice according to the package directions. Heat the oil in a wok, add the chicken strips, and cook, stirring, until brown. Using a slotted spoon, remove the chicken from the wok.

2. Add the garlic to the wok, sauté until golden, then add the bell peppers, mix well, and cook for 2–3 minutes.

3. Add the leek and chicken to the wok, then add the sugar, soy sauce, and a little vinegar and mix well. Cook for 1 minute, stirring continuously.

4. Add the rice and shrimp and cook for an additional 3 minutes.

5. Beat the eggs in a bowl with a fork. Push the rice to the edges of the wok. Add the eggs to the center of the wok and cook, carefully stirring as they solidify.

6. Mix the rice with the eggs, then add the cilantro and mix well. Drizzle the remaining vinegar over the rice.

Serve immediately in shallow bowls, garnished with the reserved cilantro.

■ Basmati rice, available in Indian grocery stores and some supermarkets, can be used instead of long-grain rice. Other good vegetables for this dish are bean sprouts, small broccoli florets, snow peas, baby corn, and bok choy.

2¼-pound pork shoulder

1 teaspoon salt
pinch of black pepper

2 tablespoons sweet paprika

1 teaspoon dried marjoram

1 tablespoon all-purpose flour,
for dusting

2 onions

3 garlic cloves

½ bunch fresh parsley sprigs

¼ cup pork lard

1 strip lemon zest

½ teaspoon caraway seeds

4 tablespoons butter, softened,
plus extra to serve

1 tablespoon tomato paste

2 cups chicken stock or
beef stock

1 pound egg noodles, prepared
according to package directions

snipped fresh chives, to garnish

Pork Goulash with Paprika & Buttered Pasta

1. Cut the pork shoulder into 1½-inch cubes. Leave the sinew and the fat on the meat–this will make the goulash tender and juicy. Put the meat into a bowl, season with the salt, pepper, paprika, and marjoram, and dust with the flour.

2. Mix together well using your hands. Cut the onions into strips. Peel and finely dice two of the garlic cloves. Tie the parsley sprigs together with string.

3. Heat the lard in a large saucepan, then add the diced garlic, followed by the onions. Gently sauté until the onions are translucent.

4. Meanwhile, finely chop the remaining garlic clove, the lemon zest, and the caraway seeds, then combine them with the butter. Chill the herb butter in the refrigerator.

5. Put the meat in the pan with the onions and gently sauté for 10 minutes, being careful not to brown it. Push the meat to the side, add the tomato paste to the center of the pan, and lightly brown. Mix it with the meat, cover the pan, and cook for an additional 10 minutes.

✳✳✳120

■ For a Szegedin goulash, add 2 cups of cooked sauerkraut and mix ⅔ cup of crème fraîche or sour cream into the goulash. Serve with freshly cooked parsley potatoes and bread dumplings.

6. Pour in the stock, replace the lid, and cook over low heat for 1 hour. Stir occasionally, adding water, if necessary. After 45 minutes, add the parsley and cook for an additional 15 minutes. Remove the parsley, add the chilled herb butter, and mix well.

Arrange the goulash on plates. Serve with pasta tossed in butter and sprinkled with chives.

3-pound leg of lamb

bunch fresh parsley

1 fresh tarragon sprig

5 shallots

2 large carrots

3 onions

1 head young cabbage

2 garlic cloves

3 Yukon Gold potatoes

2 tablespoons vegetable oil

salt and pepper, to taste

½ teaspoon tomato paste

1 bay leaf

5 cups beef stock

Irish Stew with Young Cabbage & Carrots

1. Cut into the leg of lamb along the bone and remove it carefully from the meat with the tip of your knife. Remove the fat and gristle from the skin. Cut the meat into 1¼-inch pieces. Pluck the leaves from the parsley and tarragon sprigs and set aside.

2. Cut the shallots in half, then cut the carrots diagonally into ½-inch-thick slices. Halve the onions and cut them into strips. Remove the outer leaves from the cabbage, cut it in half, remove the stem, and cut it into 1¼-inch cubes. Peel the garlic and finely chop. Peel the potatoes and cut into 1¼-inch cubes.

3. Heat the oil in a saucepan, add the garlic and then the onion strips, and cook until they are translucent. Season the meat with salt and pepper, add to the pan, and gently sauté for 10 minutes. Push the meat to the side, add the tomato paste to the center of the pan to brown it a little, then mix it with the meat. Add the bay leaf.

4. Pour the stock over the meat. You can use water as a substitute, but you will need to season the meat more if you do. Bring the stew to a boil, then simmer, covered, for 15 minutes.

120

■ Lamb shoulder can be used instead of leg of lamb, but it will have to be cooked for 15 minutes longer, because it is more marbled. The quantity of vegetables can be increased or other vegetables used according to your preference. Green beans, celery, and savoy cabbage are also delicious in this stew.

5. Add the carrots, shallots, and potatoes and simmer, covered, for an additional 10 minutes. Add the cabbage, mix all of the ingredients together, and simmer for an additional 20 minutes, then remove the bay leaf.

Finely chop the parsley and the tarragon, stir them into the pan, then serve the stew in soup bowls.

1 pound ground pork

2 tablespoons oyster sauce

1¾ cups canned coconut milk

1 teaspoon red curry paste

1 (11-ounce) can corn kernels, drained

2 tablespoons slivered almonds

Pork Meatballs in a Coconut-Curry Sauce

1. Preheat the oven to 350°F. Mix the pork with the oyster sauce and shape into small balls. Put them into a shallow ovenproof dish. Pour the coconut milk into a tall container.

2. Add the curry paste to the coconut milk and stir.

3. Using an immersion blender, blend the mixture briefly until the curry paste is thoroughly mixed in.

4. Pour the sauce over the meatballs. Sprinkle with the corn, followed by the slivered almonds, then cover with aluminum foil to prevent the almonds from burning. Cook in the preheated oven for about 25 minutes.

Transfer the meatballs to bowls and serve immediately.

*** 45

■ Milder yellow curry paste can be used instead of the red curry paste. A few young green peas can be added to the sauce, too.

10 spicy lamb sausages

2 tablespoons vegetable oil

1 garlic clove, peeled and sliced

2 onions, finely sliced

2 fresh rosemary sprigs

2 bay leaves

1⅔ cups dried white kidney beans, soaked overnight

1 teaspoon tomato paste

1 (14½-ounce) can peeled tomatoes

salt and pepper, to taste

Tomato Bean Stew with Spicy Lamb Sausage

1. Put the sausages into a saucepan with the oil and cook until brown all over. Add the garlic and cook until toasted.

2. Remove the sausages from the pan and set aside. Add the onions to the pan with the rosemary and bay leaves and cook until the onions are translucent. Push them to the side of the pan.

3. Drain and rinse the beans, then add them to the pan.

4. Add the tomato paste and tomatoes to the pan, breaking down the tomatoes with a wooden spoon. Season with salt and pepper.

5. Pour cold water over the beans until they are covered. Return the sausages to the pan, bring the mixture to a boil, boil for 10 minutes, then cover, reduce the heat, and simmer gently for 1 hour. Stir frequently, adding water as necessary to keep the beans just covered so they can cook completely.

Serve the bean stew in bowls with the lamb sausages on top.

+ 12 hours' soaking

✳
✳ 75
✳

■ Stew 2 fried duck legs, 1 strip of bacon, and a few pieces of lamb with the beans and you have a wonderful Frency-style cassoulet.

 2¼-pound lamb shoulder

salt and pepper, to taste

5 garlic cloves

2 large onions

3½ tablespoons vegetable oil

2 cinnamon sticks

6 star anise

½ teaspoon curry powder

1 teaspoon ground cumin

2 tablespoons tomato paste

1½ (14½-ounce) cans
peeled tomatoes

1½ cups basmati rice or
long-grain rice, steamed

12 saffron threads

Biryani Rice with Lamb

1. Cut the lamb into 1¼-inch cubes, then season with salt and pepper. Peel and thinly slice the garlic. Thinly slice the onion. Heat the oil in a wide saucepan. Add the garlic, cinnamon, star anise, and onions and cook for 5 minutes, until the onions are translucent. Season with salt.

2. Add the lamb and cook, stirring, until brown, then sprinkle the lamb with the curry powder and cumin. Continue to cook for an additional 10 minutes, making sure the spices don't toast too long because they can turn bitter.

3. Push the meat to the side of the pan, add the tomato paste to the center, and sauté. Add the tomatoes with their can juices and bring to a boil, then cover and cook over medium heat for about 40 minutes.

4. Use a fork to test whether the lamb is done. Remove the cinnamon sticks and the star anise and reserve to garnish.

5. Soak the saffron threads in 3½ tablespoons water, then heat until the liquid is reduced to half its volume. Spread the rice over the lamb, drizzle the water-soaked saffron over it, cover, and heat for 5 minutes.

Garnish with the reserved cinnamon sticks and star anise and serve immediately in shallow bowls.

■ Sprinkle with chopped fresh mint and serve with plain yogurt. Indian restaurants sometimes lay a few pieces of gold leaf on top of this dish.

✳
✳ 100
✳

2 heads broccoli

3 shallots

2 tomatoes

1 bunch fresh cilantro

1-inch piece fresh ginger

1 pound beef tenderloin steak

¼ cup oyster sauce

¼ cup peanut oil

1 garlic clove

pinch of sugar

juice of 1 lime

Vietnamese Beef Stew with Ginger

1. Wash the broccoli and divide it into florets, including the stems. Slice the shallots lengthwise. Cut the tomatoes into quarters, seed, and cut each quarter twice. Chop the cilantro. Peel the ginger and finely slice. Remove any fat or tendons from the beef and cut the meat into strips ¾ inch wide and 1¼ inches long. Place the beef in a bowl, combine with the oyster sauce, and marinate for 20 minutes.

2. Heat half of the oil in a nonstick wok, add the broccoli, and sauté for about 3 minutes. Move the florets to the side, then pour the remaining oil into the opposite side of the wok.

3. Chop the garlic, add to the wok, and sauté. Add the beef strips and sear for 1 minute, stirring continuously.

4. Add the shallots, ginger, and tomato pieces and toss. Sauté only briefly, so the vegetables remain crisp.

5. Add the cilantro, sugar, and lime juice. Mix once.

Transfer to bowls and serve immediately.

■ Stir in approximately 8 ounces of cellophane or wide rice noodles before serving, to create a more filling meal.

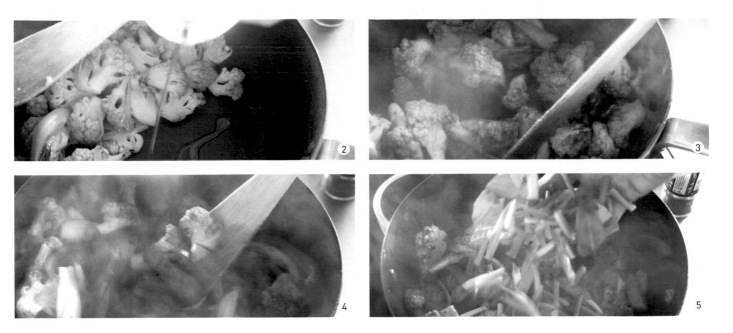

2 (2¼-pound) racks of lamb

salt and pepper, to taste

3 tablespoons olive oil

6 garlic cloves

2 fresh rosemary sprigs

2 tablespoons butter

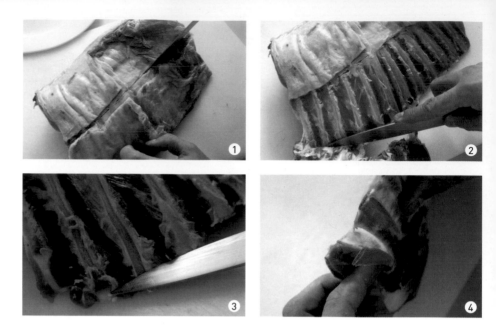

Roasted French Racks of Lamb with Rosemary

1. Put the racks of lamb on a cutting board and cut into the fatty layer at a depth of ½ inch.

2. Trim the fat and the meat from the ribs.

3. Shave the flesh off the bone with the knife, so that it is easier to remove.

4. Carefully loosen the flesh from the bone with your fingers until the bone is exposed and clean.

5. Turn it over and cut this part of the flesh off.

6. Cut along the backbone and remove the white sinew carefully. Then continue cutting on the back to the ribs.

7. Turn over again and separate the rack of lamb from the backbone with sharp kitchen shears.

8. Remove the small parts of sinew and bones from the separated rack of lamb and season it with salt and pepper on both sides.

60

✳
✳
✳

■ You can find racks of lamb that have already been trimmed to this style. Create a more elaborate crust using pecans and lemon—coarsely chop some pecan nuts, cut 2 pieces of lemon zest into fine strips, and mix them with 1 fresh rosemary sprig, 2 tablespoons of oil, and 1 teaspoon of whole-grain mustard. Coat the lamb with this mixture for the last 5 minutes of cooking.

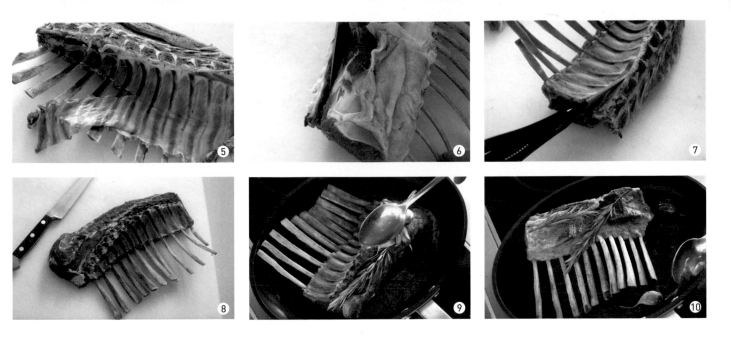

9. Preheat the oven to 350°F. Heat the oil in a wide, ovenproof skillet and put the rack of lamb in it, top-side down. Place the unpeeled garlic cloves in a bowl and press down on them with the heel of your hand. Add the garlic and the rosemary to the rack. Baste the lamb with the pan juices and turn it over after 5 minutes, replacing the rosemary on top of the rack so that it doesn't burn in the pan.

10. Add the butter and roast in the preheated oven for about 10 minutes, basting frequently.

Remove from the oven, cover with aluminum foil, and let rest for 3 minutes before serving.

- 1 large onion
- 1 pound top sirloin steak
- ½ cup vegetable oil
- 1 dried red chile
- salt and pepper, to taste
- 3 tablespoons sweet paprika
- 1 tablespoon tomato paste
- 1⅔ cups long-grain rice
- 1 cup drained canned corn kernels

Hungarian Paprikash with Corn

1. Thinly slice the onion. Slice the beef, then cut it into strips. Heat the oil in a large saucepan over medium heat, add the onions, and cook until translucent. Add the dried chile.

2. Add the beef, season with salt and pepper, sprinkle with paprika, and gently sauté. Push the beef to one side, add the tomato paste to the center of the pan, and lightly sauté to reduce the acidity.

3. Add the rice, mix well, and cook.

4. Add the corn kernels to the rice. Add 1⅔ cups water, bring to a boil, cover, and cook for about 25 minutes over medium heat. Stir occasionally, adding more water if necessary.

5. The dish is cooked when the rice has completely absorbed the liquid.

Transfer to plates and serve, sprinkled with paprika.

✳ ✳ ✳ 50

■ Beef stock can be used as a substitute for water, giving the dish more flavor. Red and yellow bell peppers, cut into strips, can also be added.

5 juniper berries

5 white peppercorns

2 onions

3 carrots

2 leeks

4 celery stalks

1 tbsp salt

2¼ pounds boneless beef chuck

2 cloves

1 bay leaf

fresh flat-leaf parsley, to garnish

snipped fresh chives, to garnish

Beef Stew with Root Vegetables & Herbs

1. Using the flat side of a knife, lightly crush the juniper berries and peppercorns.

2. Halve the unpeeled onions and cut off the root ends. Halve the carrots and cut the leeks and celery into two or three pieces, depending on their size.

3. Bring a large saucepan of lightly salted water to a boil, add the beef, and simmer for about 1 hour.

4. Add the onions, carrots, leeks, celery, juniper berries, peppercorns, cloves, and bay leaf.

5. Let simmer for an additional hour, until the meat is cooked. Remove and discard the bay leaf.

Cut the vegetables into bite-size pieces and arrange them on a serving platter with the beef. Sprinkle with parsley and chives and serve.

■ Serve with parsley potatoes, sautéed potatoes, or creamed spinach. This dish tastes delicious with tartar sauce.

* \
* **120** \
*

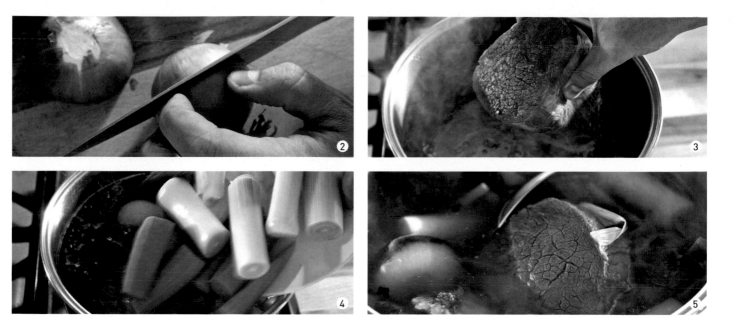

1 stick salted butter, softened

1 egg, plus 1 egg yolk

1 teaspoon chopped fresh parsley

pinch of salt

pinch of freshly grated nutmeg

½ cup self-rising flour

all-purpose flour, for dusting

9 cups chicken stock

Chicken Soup with Butter Dumplings & Nutmeg

1. Whip the butter until holding peaks. Add the egg, egg yolk, parsley, salt, and nutmeg. Beat until blended.

2. Using a rubber spatula, work in the self-rising flour and set aside for 10 minutes.

3. Use two teaspoons to shape the mixture into dumplings.

4. Put the dumplings on a board dusted with flour and chill in the refrigerator for 30 minutes.

5. Put the stock into a large saucepan, bring to a boil, and add the dumplings. Simmer until the dumplings float, then cover and let stand for 25 minutes.

Serve in soup bowls, sprinkled with nutmeg to taste.

* * * 90

■ Julienned root vegetables boiled in salted water and some chicken meat can be added to this dish. If you don't have self-rising flour, use ½ cup all-purpose flour mixed with ¾ teaspoon baking powder.

12 ounces egg noodles

⅓ cup vegetable oil

6 dried red chiles

2 carrots

½ head broccoli

2 skinless chicken breasts

2 tablespoons black bean paste

1 cup bean sprouts

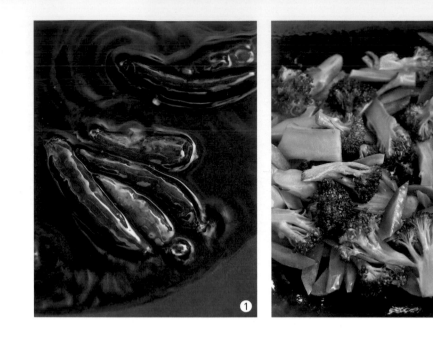

Shanghai-Style Fried Egg Noodles with Chicken

1. Cook the egg noodles according to the package directions. Heat the oil in a wok, add the chiles, and lightly brown.

2. Halve the carrots and slice diagonally. Cut the broccoli into florets. Add the carrots and broccoli to the wok and stir-fry for 3 minutes, turning frequently.

3. Cut the chicken breasts into thin strips and add to the wok. Add the black bean paste, mix, and continue stirring.

4. Add the noodles and bean sprouts, stir, and continue stir-frying.

Transfer to plates and serve immediately.

35

■ Other vegetables that go well with this dish are mushrooms, bell peppers, and bok choy.

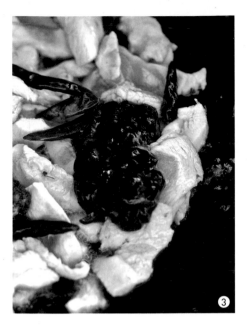

4 (8-ounce) duck breasts

2 oranges

salt and pepper, to taste

1 tablespoon vegetable oil

½ cup Cointreau

1 cup orange juice

2 tablespoons pickled green peppercorns

Roasted Duck Breast with Orange-Pepper Sauce

1. Place the duck breasts on a cutting board, skin side up. Cut off the protruding skin. Then, using a sharp knife, score the skin in a crisscross pattern.

2. Grate the orange peel using a fine grater. Use a knife to cut off all the pith from the orange, then slice the orange.

3. Season the duck breast on both sides with salt and pepper. Heat the oil in a skillet and place the breasts in the skillet skin side down.

4. Sauté the breasts over medium heat for about 10 minutes on each side, basting frequently with the duck fat. Continue to cook on the skin side until the skin is crisp.

5. Arrange the duck breasts skin side up on a serving platter and let stand. Remove the fat from the skillet, place the orange peel in the skillet, and add the Cointreau to the juices. Add the orange juice, peppercorns, and orange slices.

Serve the duck breasts on warm plates with the orange-pepper sauce.

■ Score the skin deeply to make sure that the fat escapes, otherwise the skin won't be very crisp.

*
** 35
*

1 whole duck

3 shallots, peeled

1 small apple

salt and pepper, to taste

1 garlic clove

½ bunch fresh marjoram

1 cup water

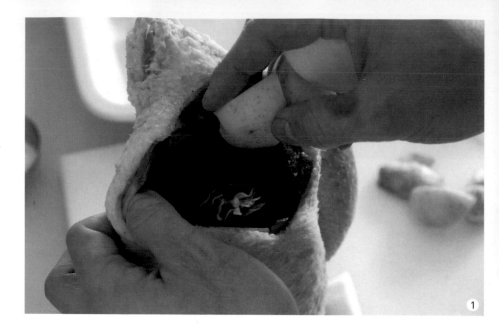

Roasted Duck with Apples

1. Ask your butcher to prepare the duck so it is ready to cook, and to pack the neck, wings, and giblets separately. Preheat the oven to 350°F. Halve the shallots. Core the apple and cut into quarters, then slice the quarters in half. Clean the inside of the duck and rub dry with paper towels. Season with salt and pepper. Stuff the duck with the unpeeled garlic clove, the shallots, the apple, and a marjoram sprig.

2. Secure the opening closed with toothpicks and tie with string. Cut off the ends of the toothpicks with scissors on both sides. This prevents the juices from oozing out during cooking and keeps the flavor in the duck. Pluck any remaining pin feathers from the skin using a pair of small pliers.

3. Season the outside of the duck with salt and pepper and rub in well.

***140

■ Serve the duck with golden potato cakes, brussels sprouts, red cabbage, or sauerkraut. Strain the cooking liquor using a fine strainer and serve as a sauce. These juices are highly concentrated, so just a little sprinkled carefully on the side of the plate should be enough.

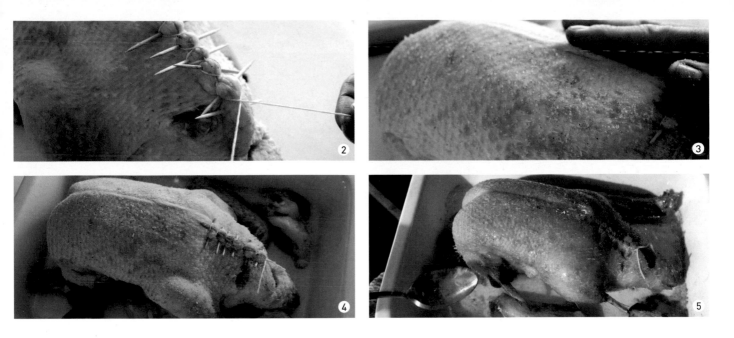

4. Place the duck and the giblets in a roasting dish. Pour in half the water and place on the lower shelf of the preheated oven.

5. Baste the duck with the cooking juices. After about 45 minutes, add the remaining water and roast the duck for an additional 45 minutes. Loosen the string with a knife and remove the toothpicks.

Place the duck on a large serving platter, garnish with marjoram sprigs, and serve.

2½ cups dried pinto beans

1 large carrot

2 celery stalks

2 garlic cloves

1 small onion

2 tablespoons olive oil

4 fresh rosemary sprigs

3 bay leaves

1 teaspoon fennel seeds, chopped

1 tablespoon tomato paste

1 cup white wine

salt and pepper, to taste

9 cups chicken stock

2 (8-ounce) duck breasts

Pinto Bean Ragout with Roasted Duck Breast

1. Soak the beans for at least 2 hours. Cut the carrots and celery into ¼-inch pieces. Crush the garlic cloves into a bowl, then dice the onions. Heat the oil in a shallow saucepan, then add the onions, carrots, and celery to the pan and gently sauté for 10 minutes.

2. Add the rosemary, bay leaves, fennel seeds, and garlic and lightly sauté.

3. Push the vegetables to one side of the pan. Add the tomato paste to the center of the pan. Add the wine and simmer to let the liquid reduce.

4. Drain and rinse the beans, add to the pan, and sauté for 2 minutes. Season with salt and pepper, pour in the chicken stock, and simmer gently for 50 minutes. Stir occasionally to prevent the beans from sticking to the bottom of the pan. Stir carefully to avoid crushing them. Add a little water if necessary.

Meanwhile, cook the duck breasts (see page 54). Divide the beans among four serving plates, then slice the duck breasts, arrange on top of the beans, and serve immediately.

■ Fennel seeds are easier to chop if you drizzle them with a little oil beforehand to prevent them from jumping. The pinto bean ragout also goes well with pork or lamb sausages.

4 (9-ounce) pigeons

4 slices of white bread

1 shallot

½ bunch fresh parsley

1 stick butter, softened

2 eggs

salt and pepper, to taste

pinch of freshly grated nutmeg

8 bacon strips

4 garlic cloves

10 juniper berries

2 tablespoons vegetable oil

4 fresh rosemary sprigs

Stuffed Pigeons Wrapped in Bacon

1. Ask your butcher to prepare the pigeons so they are ready to cook and to pack the heart and liver separately. To make the stuffing, finely cube the heart and liver. Remove the crusts from the white bread and cut the bread into ¼-inch cubes. Finely chop the shallot and the parsley. Beat the butter in a bowl until it is fluffy. Separate the eggs and add the yolks to the butter, one at a time. Season with salt and pepper. Add the nutmeg and mix with a wire whisk, then add the shallot and parsley.

2. Add the liver, heart, and bread cubes and mix carefully.

3. Rub the inside of the pigeons with paper towels and remove any skin and blood residues. Season inside and out with salt and pepper and fill with the stuffing.

4. Wrap each of the pigeons with two bacon strips and tie together with string. Using the flat side of a knife, crush the unpeeled garlic and the juniper berries.

5. Preheat the oven to 425°F. Heat the oil in an ovenproof skillet and place the pigeons, rosemary, juniper berries, and garlic in the skillet. Cook on one side until brown, then turn and brown on the other side. Transfer to the preheated oven and cook for about 25 minutes, frequently basting with the juices. Remove from the oven, take off the string, and halve the pigeons lengthwise using a sharp knife.

Arrange on plates and serve immediately.

■ Place any excess stuffing in a buttered soufflé dish and bake in the oven for about 15 minutes at 400°F. The butter makes it easier to turn out the stuffing later. Pumpkin gratin and salsify root, which is also called vegetable oyster, make wonderful accompaniments for the pigeon dinner.

*
* 90
*

1 garlic bulb

1 lemon

bunch fresh parsley

4 (12-ounce) Cornish game hens

salt and pepper, to taste

10 ounces shallots

4 tablespoons butter

Cornish Game Hens Roasted with Lemon & Garlic

1. Preheat the oven to 350°F. Set the garlic, stem upright, on a work surface and press down with the palm of your hand to loosen the cloves. Remove the outer skin and crush the cloves in their skins. Rinse the lemon under hot water and cut into ¼-inch slices. Pluck the parsley off the stems. Wash the Cornish game hens and dry them inside with paper towels.

2. Thoroughly season the hens, inside and out, with salt and pepper. Stuff with the pressed garlic cloves and the parsley, reserving some of the parsley to garnish.

3. Place the stuffed hens in a roasting pan. Cut off the stem end of the shallots but do not peel. Arrange the shallots around the hens. Distribute the butter over the hens.

4. Roast for 25 minutes in the preheated oven. Add ½ cup of water to the pan and scrape the bottom with a wooden spoon to loosen the sediment. Add the lemon slices. Baste the hens with the juices and roast for an additional 15 minutes. Remove from the oven.

Serve the hens with the shallots and juices, garnished with the remaining parsley.

■ Be careful not to injure the skin when you pluck the remaining pin feathers with a pair of fish bone pliers or other small pliers. The white meat would dry out at these spots. Cornish game hens taste just as delicious cold. Serve with any type of potato dish.

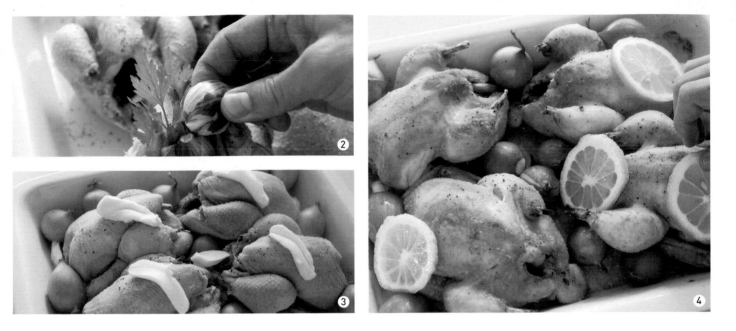

INDEX